Successful Small Business
Marketing Made Easy!

Successful Small Business Marketing Made Easy!

✦

A No Nonsense Approach To Profiting In Any Market!

John A. Schneider

iUniverse, Inc.
New York Lincoln Shanghai

Successful Small Business Marketing Made Easy!
A No Nonsense Approach To Profiting In Any Market!

Copyright © 2007 by John A. Schneider

iUniverse books may be ordered through booksellers or by contacting:

iUniverse
2021 Pine Lake Road, Suite 100
Lincoln, NE 68512
www.iuniverse.com
1-800-Authors (1-800-288-4677)

Because of the dynamic nature of the Internet, any Web addresses or links contained in this book may have changed since publication and may no longer be valid.

The views expressed in this work are solely those of the author and do not necessarily reflect the views of the publisher, and the publisher hereby disclaims any responsibility for them.

ISBN: 978-0-595-45098-5 (pbk)
ISBN: 978-0-595-89409-3 (ebk)

Printed in the United States of America

Contents

Introduction

Why write a book about small business marketing? Two reasons, really.

When I graduated college in the late 1980's and the economy was in a recession, I experienced a real world jolt I didn't expect. In short, I found myself with a college diploma in hand and little else. Like most graduates in similar situations, I attempted to land a job through traditional means: I answered help wanted ads and networked. As the months passed and the prospects of landing a position looked bleak, I decided to take matters into my own hands. Although I was working part-time, my bank account was dwindling.

Bent on reaching a decision maker, I marched into the local newspaper and purchased a display ad targeted towards readers of high net worth. My reasoning? These people were successful because they were decision makers in their respective organizations. And even if they weren't decision makers regarding marketing, I thought they might be impressed by my bravado and forward my ad to an HR person (or so I hoped!). I sat down with an advertising account executive at the paper and made my first advertising purchase.

Although the paper was only a weekly, I was enthusiastic about the possibilities. The sales rep suggested I run the ad at least three times, but I wouldn't listen. I figured the salespeople were trying to take what little money I had, and I wasn't about to get suckered into making a multiple-week buy! I couldn't imagine how the beautiful ad I created wouldn't be a home-run. The ad itself was simple—it contained a headshot of myself, along with a short message about who I was and the kind of position I desired. I rented a post office box in town and waited for the responses.

The first week saw no responses—I'm sure you can imagine my reaction! It was bad enough I was going to lose what little money I had on this idea, but to have no responses was unforgivable!

I marched into the newspaper and spoke with the local sales rep, and she encouraged me to run the ad again. "Are you kidding me?" I asked. Aggravated and desperate, I gave it another go. Little did I know at the time that I had just learned my first lesson in advertising. (Frequency and consistency are vital to creating awareness.)

That next week, I received four letters of inquiry, each asking me to come in for an interview. One of the interviews was with a local newspaper—selling ADVERTISING! Excited, I took the position, which started a career for me that led to my working in advertising and sales for the next 17 years. During that time, I sold advertising to large and small companies. I worked in advertising agencies, newspapers, online companies—you name it. I bought advertising, sold advertising, and created advertising before starting my own business. During that time, I worked with small businesses.

The reason why I'm so dedicated and excited about small businesses is simple: Small businesses are the backbone of our economy. Despite the headlines in the business section of newspapers and the news coming from financial channels that scream about the fortunes made or lost by the Fortune 500, small businesses make up over 51% of the American Gross Domestic Product (GDP)[*].

What's more, small businesses have a more personal meaning for me. Most of my family members own their own business, so I have seen, firsthand, the hard work that goes into building a business. The long hours and stress come alongside a sense of pride and independence that are hard to find in the world of big business.

More importantly, however, I saw small business start-ups at the development level. Every week, I was on the phone with a new business startup looking to start advertising. Consequently, I saw new businesses grow and thrive, while others just withered away. I watched established businesses go under while new businesses grew rapidly. And now that I'm a business owner myself, I understand both sides and can appreciate the role effective advertising plays in the success of a business.

Of course, there are many reasons why some businesses thrive while others fail, and those are beyond the scope of this book. But one factor that makes a positive difference in the success of any business is having an intimate knowledge of the

---

[*]   "The Facts About Small Business," U.S. Small Business Administration Office of Advocacy, August 2000

target market. Understanding your market and how to cultivate it makes for effective marketing and advertising.

What to expect

My goal in writing this book is to make your business successful by showing you, the business owner, how to give your business the maximum quality exposure for the least amount of money.

Successful Small Business Marketing Made Easy! is laid out in a step-by-step manner which allows you to develop an effective marketing campaign—regardless of experience. Whether you're a business novice looking to start a new business or an experienced professional looking to improve your business, this book will help you grow your business through proven marketing techniques. Each chapter will present questions about your business from a marketing perspective. By the time you finish this book, you will have a clear game plan in hand that will put you on the path to earning the kind of money you envisioned for your business.

A Word About Written Exercises

The temptation that will arise while reading this book will either be to answer the questions in your mind and move on or ignore them altogether in order to save time. I strongly encourage you to take the time to write down each question and record your own answer!

Why is this important? By writing down specific answers to the questions, you will be taking fuzzy notions and ideas and making them concrete. The best way to take an idea and make it a reality is to put it in physical form. By writing down specifics, you'll be creating a physical roadmap that will do two very important things: keep your advertising campaign on track and direct you to where you need to be. This will be invaluable as you make marketing decisions down the road.

Just as recording financial transactions in a ledger is important to the financial health of your business, so, too, is a marketing plan. As such, you should allocate a portion of your business time exclusively to advertising and marketing, which will create distinct records of your marketing campaign.

How To Use This Book

Successful Small Business Marketing Made Easy! is written in sequence, so skipping around initially is discouraged. Once you complete this book, you will undoubtedly want to revisit sections you may have questions about. Over time, it will become a useful reference that will assure you that your marketing campaign is on track.

Marketing has increasingly become a complicated field of study, even for small businesses. *Successful Small Business Marketing Made Easy!* is designed to be a basic primer to help the small business owner, unfamiliar with marketing, build his or her business in a smart, straight-forward manner. At the conclusion of this book, there will be a section of recommended reading for those interested in learning more.

Now, let's start making money by putting together a profitable marketing plan for your business!

1

Marketing and Your Business

OK, so you've plunked down your hard-earned money for a book about marketing, thinking "I hope this thing can help me get some new customers," or "I know I need to sell my product or service—but where do I start?" Regardless of the reason for the purchase, you acknowledge the need for a plan that will connect your business with your target audience. You want to let people know you have something to offer. What's more, you want them to choose you before anyone else within your line of work.

By deciding you want to learn more about connecting with your potential customer base, you've already taken a step towards making strong sales a reality.

What Exactly is Marketing?

In its most basic sense, marketing is the process of communicating your product or service to the public, or a segment of the public. While this sounds simple enough, the process can be a bit daunting if you have never put together a marketing campaign before. What exactly should you do? How should you do it? Should you advertise? Just thinking about these questions causes many small business owners to throw up their arms in frustration!

But, the fact remains that marketing doesn't have to be complicated. All it requires is a little organization on your part, along with having a solid grasp of what your business represents and what it has to offer. Sometimes, there is more to what you do than what you envision, but this is where marketing has to start. To find out what you specifically offer to your audience, we've provided a series of short exercises to help you answer these questions in a clear, concise way, which will help you reach your goal.

What's the Difference between Marketing and Advertising?

As mentioned earlier, the simplest explanation of marketing is the communication of your product or service. This can take the form of sales promotions, public relations, personal selling, and advertising. Advertising is the process of communicating what you have to offer by purchasing media space. As you'll see, there is a difference.

Why Marketing is Important

Imagine having a dream of throwing one of the biggest parties ever. You spend enormous amounts of time scouting out locations, auditioning bands that play a wide variety of music, acquiring tables and chairs, and choosing the finest cutlery for place settings. You spend time pouring over menus and even more time buying decorations. In the process, you spend thousands and thousands of dollars.

Now, imagine no one showing up because no invitations were sent.

Sound crazy? Well, many small businesses make this same kind of mistake when they decide not to actively market their business. The economic environment in today's competitive world demands more from you, a business owner, than just opening the doors for business. You need to make your case consistently to your target market if you hope to grow your business for the long term.

Common Misconceptions

More than any other discipline, marketing suffers from a myriad of misconceptions. Here are a few of the more common ones I've encountered over the years as an advertising sales rep:

- I don't have the money

- Advertising doesn't work

- I don't need to market my business; word of mouth will carry me

- I'll advertise once I start to make some money

- I won't advertise until the economy turns around

- I want to market my company, but I don't know how

- Business is good; I don't need to advertise

- I have too much business—why market?

- I've been here for __ years; everyone knows me

- Advertising costs too much money

- I don't have time to advertise

- TV. Radio. Print. Direct Mail. Plus 3 or 4 other community sponsorships. Where do I start?

- People in my line of work don't advertise

- Marketing is too expensive

Do any of these sound familiar? Chances are great that you may have said some of the same things yourself about marketing and advertising. Some of these statements do raise valid questions. But, for the most part, these statements simply aren't true (unless your business fundamentals are flawed, for example). After reading this book, you'll see why these statements and the mindset projected through these thoughts are hindrances to effectively running a successful business.

The Truth about Marketing and Advertising

For most business owners, marketing ranks right up there with paying taxes and bills—stuff that is needed to run a business but that takes time away from actually conducting business. Unlike taxes and bills, however, many business owners simply choose to avoid marketing—a fatal mistake.

Marketing is the lifeblood of a company. Funneling new customers into your business to replace customers who either move or leave for some other reason is a natural part of the business cycle. Thus, marketing is crucial to not only replacing these customers but to build your customer base as well. Without marketing, the odds of running a successful business decrease substantially.

Effective marketing accomplishes three important things. Its goals are to:

1. Create awareness about your business

2. Induce potential customers to try your business

3. Insure that your existing customers will continue doing business with you

That's it. That's the goal of marketing in a nutshell. Now, let's start putting together a revenue-generating marketing plan specific to your product or service that will bring or maintain success for your business!

2

Who Are You? Establishing an Identity

Perhaps the most important yet overlooked part of marketing resides in answering one question: Who are you?

Developing A Mission Statement

Developing a valid mission statement is crucial before marketing. Why? Simply put, a mission statement will set the tone of your marketing campaign. It will be a statement of why your business is in existence to begin with.

A mission statement, in the basic sense, is a statement of purpose. A mission statement should not be confused with a financial goal, however. Here's an example of an effective mission statement for a software designer:

The purpose of XYZ is to provide clients with software that will help their business better deliver goods and services to their customers. We do this by providing the insight and technical knowledge needed to make their business successful.

While the above example highlights the mission of a software designer, it could just as easily apply to a landscaper, card shop, or any other business.

A mission statement shouldn't be too wordy or convoluted, nor should it be a meaningless collection of thoughts put together just for the sake of having a mission statement.

Exercise

1. Take a moment and write a mission statement for your company. Why are you engaged in this business? Keep in mind that a good mission statement goes beyond earning just dollars—it acknowledges servicing people and making their life better. If you already have one, take this opportunity to review and revise it.

Your mission statement should be placed on an index card or some place where you can refer to it during a business day. It's an excellent way to insure that your business decisions are in sync with who you are as a business. Your mission statement should be reviewed periodically to see that it is still valid.

Since this is a book about small business marketing, we won't spend much time on the mechanics of putting together a successful mission statement. If you are interested in learning more about developing a mission statement, look to your local library or bookstore for books on the subject. **It's not an exaggeration to say that a mission statement is an essential ingredient to running a successful business, and is crucial for putting together an effective marketing campaign.**

Why? Because how you see yourself and your business will be an important part of the marketing message you create.

Developing a Business Brand

How is your business perceived?

Believe it or not, many marketing professionals—some with MBA degrees who are working in Fortune 500 corporate marketing departments and high-end advertising agencies—fail to ask this very simple question, which has led to the loss of millions of dollars, failed product lines, and lost jobs.

Your business philosophy will shape your business identity, or brand. Branding has been a hot topic in the marketing world in recent years, as companies attempt to stand out from the competition in a very cluttered marketplace. Walk into any bookstore. There are shelves and shelves of books devoted to the subject of branding and filled with theories and cutting edge research on the subject.

The purpose of a business brand is to establish a unique identity in the marketplace through the use of both graphic images and the written word. Most businesses—small businesses, in particular—fail to pay attention to what they offer that others don't. What's more, some businesses actually go out of their way to copy other businesses!

Why is a unique identity important? The average person is exposed to literally hundreds of advertisements in a day. The best way to stand out is to establish an identity that communicates your understanding of the needs and wants of your prospective clients. For a small business, failure to establish a clear identity can be fatal. Yet small marketing budgets and competitive business environments make establishing a presence in the marketplace a challenge.

Exercises

The following four questions are designed to assist you in developing a *brand*. When answering these questions, be as specific as possible. Take your time answering the following questions:

1. Why are you starting a business?

2. What is it you do? Be as specific as possible.

3. Are you looking to service the high, middle, or low end of your market?

4. What are the demographics of your potential audience (geographic, gender, etc.)? Who do you want to reach with your business?

5. What image do you want to convey? Relaxed? Creative? Trustworthy? Fun?

Customer Service

Customer service is an important part of any successful brand. It's no secret that customer service (providing or not providing a good or service and the manner in which you provide it) is at the heart of whether or not a business succeeds or fails. Interesting point, you may say to yourself, but how does this relate to marketing?

Case Study

Once, when I was working as an advertising rep for a local newspaper, I made a presentation to a local optometrist, selling the benefit of advertising. It was my first big sale for the newspaper, and I was thrilled! One of the client's major challenges was to build market share. His biggest competitor owned a large chunk of the local market and advertised heavily in all the local papers, billboards, and phone directories. Everywhere you turned, he was there!

When I sat down with my new client, I had only one question: "What makes you different from him?"

After fumbling for answers, my client acknowledged that very little differentiated them. Eyeglasses were priced the same, he explained, and both of them offered ophthalmology services as well—also commonplace in the industry. His location next to a large national retailer in a popular shopping plaza provided him with plenty of traffic, although that same national retailer also offered similar products—and services at a lower price.

Finally, he delivered an answer I've heard time and time again. "Service," he said, "is what separates my business from the others in town." After asking him a set of detailed questions like those you just answered, we put together an advertising campaign based on his business philosophy. And, with a new business philosophy in hand, we put together a new advertising campaign, which worked well for the first three months.

After that time, he became sidetracked from the original store and began spending more time at a new store he opened. Without him at his original store, service began to fade. According to his records, most new customers he won over from his competitors began disappearing.

Although he acknowledged his lack of attention to service, he asserted in frustration that "advertising didn't work," although there was no reason to believe that the advertising medium that pinpointed his target market suddenly stopped working for no reason. Ultimately, as his attention to service waned further, so did his businesses.

The lesson to be learned? Far too many small business owners claim to deliver excellent customer service when, in reality, the service they provide is simply average or poor. Business owners who maintain their focus on serving and making customer service the centerpiece of their marketing strategy undoubtedly win in the marketplace.

Excercise
1. What service can you offer that no one else in your market offers? Take a moment and write it down.

Simply put, marketing doesn't end when a potential client calls you or walks into your business. You need to fulfill their needs, and do it in a manner that makes the experience enjoyable. That is what will insure their return visits and provide tangible proof that you are true to the image you portray.

Remember—You are Your Brand!

Marketing is the communication of who you are. We live in a competitive society, and there are other people who perform the same (or similar) kind of work or product you are looking to provide. Why should people choose you over others? While price may or may not be a factor, one thing is certain: It's your brand that will set you apart from others. People are willing to pay more for a product or service they can receive elsewhere (for less) if their experience is enjoyable. Here's a list of qualities that potential customers look for in a business:

1. Friendliness

2. Punctuality

3. Dependability

4. Trustworthiness

5. Comfort

6. Honesty

If you think this sounds elementary, you're right! Yet how many businesses actually adhere to this philosophy? Sadly, very few. The experience you create for the customer will play a large role in your success or failure. Again, people will pay more and go out of their way for a product or service that provides them with an enjoyable experience.

Case Study

When I first moved to Florida, I opened a bank account at a bank that had just opened in the area. In addition to offering rates that beat the pants off all the other local banks, this bank had great service. What's more, the tellers at the bank knew my name when I came in with my banking business.

All that began to change three years after I opened my account. Service began to decline, and new tellers began to appear who were less friendly (and didn't remember my name!). After two bad experiences, I closed my account. In the months that followed, I spoke with other people who had become disillusioned with the bank as well.

At about the time I closed the account, the company rolled out a multi-million dollar advertising campaign in an attempt to grow its business. Clearly, this is an example of a company fighting itself by driving clients away while trying to lure new business.

When there's a discrepancy between a company's marketing message and actual practice, you can "take it to the bank" that customers will look elsewhere.

Lesson: Be honest about who you are and what you can deliver. If there is a discrepancy between the two, marketing will not be able to save you!

Exercise

1. Think about a business you enjoy frequenting. It could be a restaurant, mechanic, even a physician! What is it you like about the business? About the people who serve you? Take a minute to jot down your thoughts.

A Final Word

A successful brand will not only differentiate you from your competition, it will guide the marketing message you present to the public. Take the time to develop a solid brand before moving forward with your marketing campaign.

3

Finding Your Target Market

The most important questions to ask as a business owner should revolve around your target market. Too often, small businesses and businesses in general take a ready-shoot-aim approach to marketing. The amount of marketing dollars that are wasted due to failure to answer this question is staggering.

Perhaps you've made this mistake yourself. If you have, don't feel bad! Many experienced marketers (this author included!) have made this mistake in the rush to profit from a money-making idea.

Finding your target market needn't be a headache. It does, however, require some thought. Remember, the point of any marketing campaign is to connect with customers and prospective customers. If you spend time and money targeting the wrong market segment (opening a snowmobile store in Florida, for example) will yield frustration and disappointment!

Exercises

Here are some important questions to ask before embarking on your marketing campaign:

1. Are you marketing to men? Women? Both?

2. What age group are you targeting?

3. Are you looking to target a specific demographic area?

4. Are you looking to target people with a specific interest?

5. Are you marketing to other businesses or the general public?

6. What are the buying habits of your target market?

7. What is the average budget or income of your target market?

This isn't an exhaustive list, and I encourage you to come up with as many questions pertaining to your market as possible. Answering this list of questions will provide you with a solid foundation before embarking on your marketing campaign. **In addition to greatly improving your profit potential, answers to these questions will help clarify where you will market and how much to spend on marketing.**

Don't be afraid to use the resources available to you to learn more about your market. Professional organizations are an excellent place to start. Of course, the Internet is a great tool as well.

Your public library has loads of information that can help you define your target market and show you what industry leaders are doing. If you can't find what you want, don't be afraid to ask librarians for help. Oftentimes, I've been surprised to learn about resources I didn't know existed both online and in print when I've asked for assistance in locating materials.

A Final Word

Targeting your core market is perhaps the most important task of a business owner. Lack of information will cost you in more ways than one.

At the same time, be aware of "information paralysis." There is such a thing as having so much information that you loose sight of whom your target market is.

Worse yet is doing nothing because you still need more information. If you feel you have a good handle on your market, it's time to move forward.

You may find along the way that you have misread the market, or that your target market changes due to external factors (technology, state of the economy, demographic changes). Because the marketplace is fluid, reassessing your market from time to time is important.

4

Putting Together a Marketing Budget

Okay. You've put together a business philosophy statement and a business brand. You've zeroed in on your target market. Congratulations! You've already stepped to the front of the marketing success line!

Before you truly get started, however, there are some basic questions you need to answer. They may seem obvious, and in some cases, silly. But, as with the case of branding, answering these questions can make all the difference when it comes to putting together a successful marketing program.

Pricing

One of the core questions you need to establish before setting a marketing budget surrounds pricing. Regardless of whether you sell a product or service, establishing a price structure is a must before moving forward with a budget.

There is no one way to set pricing. However, the traditional *cost plus pricing* model usually serves as a popular method of pricing.

Cost Plus Pricing = (cost of product + gross profit) + overhead = Sale Price

Once pricing is established, you can not only build a comprehensive marketing budget, but also figure your rate of return on your marketing dollars.

How Much Should You Spend?

As an advertising sales rep, one of the first questions I ask a potential client after learning about his/her business is the following:

"How much are you looking to spend?"

Predictably, the response I get is a resounding, "As little as possible," followed by a slight grin!

As a business owner, you have to put money out to secure a place of business: government licenses, inventory, employees, office equipment, business equipment, and taxes. Establishment of a business will also probably require you to sink a sizeable amount of your own money into the start-up venture. When you add in the loans, the pressure to succeed is enormous (I can see your head shaking, "Yes!"). So, it's understandable that business owners want to spend as little as possible outside of what is deemed as necessary.

Small business owners often make the fatal mistake of not including advertising when putting together their business plans for the fiscal year. Often times, deciding when and how much to spend on marketing is done by the seat of their pants—and out of any of the "leftover" funds. As you will see, this a mistake.

Seriously, How Much Should You Spend?

You'll be happy to know that this is a question that some of the largest businesses in the world ask, so it's not just a question for the small businessperson!

One school of thought is that a business should spend between 2% to 5% of its gross revenue on advertising—4% to 10% of gross revenue if the business is new. The second school of thought is that each industry has what is considered a "standard" amount that businesses typically spend on advertising. Here are a few sample categories:

Retail Stores
Auto Services
Financial Services
Landscape Services
Computer Specialists
Attorneys
Freelance Writers

Exercises

1. What is your annual projected gross sales?

2. What is considered the normal marketing budget for your industry? (The answer to this question can be given in an actual dollar range or a percent of projected annual gross revenue.)

Calculating a Minimum—Maximum Marketing Budget

Perhaps the best approach to budgeting involves calculating a minimum and maximum budget. Here's how it works:

1. Take 10% and 12% of your projected annual gross sales and multiply each by the mark-up on your average transaction. (Remember, we're talking about gross mark-up, not margin.)

2. Deduct your rent from the adjusted 10-percent-of-sales number and the adjusted 12-percent-of-sales number.

3. The remaining balances represent the minimum and maximum allowable advertising budget for the year.

Example

Let's assume your business is projected to generate $100,000 in sales this year, a profit margin of 40%, with rent at $6,000 for the year.

Step 1: Calculate 10% and 12% of sales

10% = $10,000
12% = $12,000

Step 2: Convert the profit margin into mark-up

$$\frac{\text{Profit Margin}}{\text{Cost}} = \frac{\$40,000}{\$50,000} = 80\% \text{ Mark-Up}$$

Step 3: Multiply the low and high end of the budget by 80%

$10,000 x .80 = $8,000
$12,000 x .80 = $9,600

Step 4: Deduct Rent

$8,000 - $6,000 = $2,000
$9,600 - $6,000 = $3,600

Marketing Budget

Thus, the advertising budget (using this method) is between $2,000 on the low end and $3,600 on the high end.

Many believe that failure to take mark-up and rent into consideration when putting together an advertising budget creates an unrealistic number, and I agree. This gives you a good starting place.

Other Methods of Budgeting

Lifetime Value of A Customer

1. Calculate customers' average monthly spending. This can be found by using the following formula:

   Average Monthly Sales
   Total Number of Active Customers

2. Calculate the average lifetime of a customer.

   Compare current customers from a past period. Then, find out what time period you would have lost 50% of your original customers. The resulting number is the average lifetime of your customers.

3. Multiply lifetime value by the average dollar amount of sales. This is the lifetime value of a customer.

4. Deduct direct costs from that figure (costs you wouldn't have if you didn't sell to customers)

5. Average the Gross Contribution

6. The resulting number is the amount you can spend to acquire each new customer and improve your business profits.

Example

Now, let's put the formula to work with an example!

1. Let's first calculate the customers' average spending. For the sake of example, let's assume the average monthly sale is $25,000, and total number of customers is 50.

$$\frac{25,000}{50} \quad = \quad \$500$$

So, the average customer spent $500 purchasing your goods or services.

2. Let's assume that, after comparing current customers with past customers, you come up with 2.5 years.

3. Now, let's multiply the lifetime by the average amount spent:

$500 x 12 (months) x 2.5 years = $15,000

4. Great! We now have the lifetime value of a customer—but we're not done yet. Remember, we need to deduct direct costs, such as delivery fees and cost of product.

Cost of product delivery	$40
Cost of sold items	$600
Total Direct Cost	$640

5. Finally, let's subtract the direct cost from the lifetime value of the customer:

$$\$15,000 - \$640 = \$14,360$$

The average gross contribution is $14,360. That means you can spend a minimum of $14,360 to acquire a new customer. If you spend less, you make money. If you spend more, you lose money.

This is just an example of this formula in action—you can plug in your own numbers. If you're just starting out, you may want to wait for a time before using this formula, unless you have solid numbers to apply.

Unit of Sales

The unit of sales method of calculating a marketing budget revolves around one basic question: How much advertising is needed to sell each unit? For example, if you run a hardware store and know that it will cost .06 of advertising to sell a bag of grass seed, then it will cost $480 to sell 8,000 bags of grass seed.

There are other, more complex methods of allocating money for advertising, but the methods outlined above should provide you with a good start.

The Best Kept Secret In Marketing: Co-Op Money

Oftentimes manufacturers will pay either part or all of an advertising campaign as an incentive for businesses to advertise their products. Usually these programs are not well publicized, so make sure you ask the manufacturers of products you sell if they have a co-op program. Needless to say, this can help with your budget.

Final Word

Although there are other techniques that businesses use to establish marketing budgets, the approaches outlined in this chapter are the easiest and most popular among business owners. Keep in mind that the budget you establish for marketing will, by and large, play a role in the media you will use.

5

Setting Marketing Objectives and Measuring Results

Now that you've set up a marketing budget, you're ready to start marketing, right?

Not yet!

The only thing worse than not setting up a marketing budget is not measuring the effectiveness of the marketing campaign you are funding. Before you spend a dime on marketing, it is essential that you establish a way to measure its effectiveness.

Back in the days when I sold advertising to small retail businesses, the one complaint I heard most frequently regarding advertising was "it doesn't work." More often than not, the reason business owners came to this conclusion was due to a lack of measurement or the expectation of unrealistic goals. Of course, there are times when even a measured campaign will not deliver reasonable results, and we'll take a look at the reasons for that later.

Case Study

As an advertising sales rep, two of my primary jobs were to approach a business with the intent of finding out what their needs were and how I could help them. This was the case with a local hardware store.

The owner, a crusty old gentleman, always responded to my inquiries about advertising with the same answer: "It doesn't work." Needless to say, I was anxious to prove him wrong!

After a few calls, he finally agreed to advertise in a special section of the paper dedicated to a local event. The business card size ad, which contained a coupon for a $12.99 item, cost the hardware storeowner a grand total of $32.00.

Afterwards, I checked in with him to see how the response was to the ad. "Terrible," he replied. "We didn't get any results from the ad."

Fortunately, the man's son, who managed the store, happened to be pricing goods a few steps away. When he heard his father mention he didn't get results, he quickly interjected. "Actually," he said, "we received 11 coupons so far."

Working a quick Return-On-Investment formula, the customer realized a profit of $110.89 and a 347% return on investment. In addition to the high rate of return, the customer didn't figure on the other items the coupon user probably purchased (which also contributed to the advertiser's bottom line) as well as the lifetime value of the new customers who were attracted by the advertisement. All in all, not bad for running one small ad just one time! Or, so you would think. The customer never advertised with me again, still claiming that advertising didn't work!

The above story highlights an important issue when it comes to advertising and marketing in general, and that's the issue of expectations.

What Do You Want to Accomplish?

Before you decide to advertise, it's important to first decide what you want to accomplish: Monthly sales to increase by 12 percent? The sales of 75 air conditioning units? An increase in the number of weekly billable hours? Regardless of the objective, you first need to have it clearly set in your mind what you want to accomplish. Putting a measurable number together is the first step towards measuring effectiveness. This will help determine if your advertising is hitting your target audience.

What is Your Timeline?

The next question you need to answer is timeline. Do you want to increase sales in a one- or two-week period? One month? Six months? Attaching a time frame to a campaign is important as well.

One of the objectives you should set is an advertising schedule. For example, if you are in the ice cream business, you'll spend the bulk of your advertising during the summer, with late spring/early fall a quick second. Most likely, you will do little advertising in the winter months. The same holds true for other seasonal businesses, such as air conditioning or landscaping.

Web designers, however, may find they have to advertise year 'round. A florist may advertise heavily from Thanksgiving to Easter. For business owners in tourist areas, the bulk of advertising will take place "in season." **Regardless of your business, plan to spend the bulk of your advertising budget during your busy season.**

A Word for New Businesses

New business owners face a challenge not experienced by more established businesses: the entrance into a marketplace where competition already exists. If your business is truly unique, you may have to educate your target market about how your product or service will benefit them.

Either way, new business owners should plan on marketing expenditures that will allow them to compete for the desired target audience. Because the public is bombarded with hundreds of ads in an average day, just getting through to your target audience will require more initial expenditures.

Ultimately, you want to achieve what is considered the Holy Grail of marketing: Top Of Mind awareness. The concept of Top of Mind awareness was popularized in the landmark book written by Al Ries and Jack Trout called *Positioning: The Battle For Your Mind.*

The need to establish yourself means you should have an aggressive marketing plan for the first 12 months of your business. This doesn't necessarily mean high expenditures for the whole year—simply an aggressive, overall marketing effort.

Exercises

1. Take a moment to think about the sales goals for your business. What do you want to accomplish? Make sure to answer this question in numeric form (i.e., "I'd like to increase my sales by 8%."). Be realistic.

2. Now ask yourself the time frame in which you want to accomplish this goal. Take a moment, and write it down. Again, be realistic!

Tracking Your Marketing Responses

Setting an objective is meaningless unless there's a mechanism to measure progress. Here's a list of measurement techniques you can use:

1. Calls—Some businesses set up special phone numbers they only publicize in advertising. They know any calls coming in on that number are a direct result of the campaign.

2. Coupons—A great way to measure the effectiveness of advertising in print is the use of coupons. Caution should be used, however; some customers may not be comfortable cashing in coupons or may forget to bring them. Inquiries about a specific promotion should be noted and matched up with coupons redeemed.

3. Sales—If you advertise a specific washing machine, and sales of that machine increase, you can reasonably assume your advertising campaign was responsible.

4. Number of Responses Mailed In—Popular with direct mail.

5. Website Clicks and Conversions—With Internet advertising becoming more and more of a dominating force, the amount of clicks an Internet ad receives can easily be measured. Best of all, the total number of these clicks that result in sales (conversions) can provide you with great feedback.

6. Ask!—This is the best way to measure response ... and yet the least used. Usually, business owners feel that, by asking, they may be making buyers feel uncomfortable. And that's understandable. In today's world, we all feel uncomfortable with the amount of information asked of us from business.

One method a customer of mine used was quite effective. After initially greeting the customer, assisting them if needed, and completing the sale, they would innocently ask how they heard of his business. Usually, it goes something like this: "Out of curiosity, how did you hear about us?"

People are normally upfront with their answers when asked this question *after* their purchase. Resistance comes when people feel like they are being held hostage to give information before a purchase, leading to flippant and sometimes deliberately misleading information. Having a casual approach after the sale is completed will yield more accurate responses. When people call to inquire about your business, answer all their questions first and, then, at the end of the conversation, nonchalantly inquire of them how they heard of your business.

Other Methods

Tracking advertising has become a very hot topic as more and more businesses look to justify advertising expenditures. Some businesses try to find out as much information as possible to make their advertising efforts as effective as possible. Requiring certain types of information (addresses and zip codes, phone numbers, and even using cookies on your website) are all methods that advertisers have utilized to become knowledgeable about customers and their responses to advertising.

A word to the wise: Be careful not to alienate clients by being too probing. More and more, people resent many forms of tracking that look to unearth personal information. Watch what you do!

Case Study

One of the most successful advertisers I worked with was a landscaper who had been in the area for some 18 years. In addition to a unique way of advertising, my client had daily sheets listing all the places he advertised in, and had his receptionist ask all new callers how they heard about the company. She would then place a mark under whatever media outlet given by the potential customer. This provided a very effective way to track responses and measure the effectiveness of existing advertising campaigns, right down to the day and date.

Measuring Responses

Once you've tracked your responses, convert them into numbers, so you will have a benchmark for measurement. While there are many methods and formulas to use, we'll focus on some of the most useful and common methods of measurement.

Return-On-Investment (ROI)

By far the most popular, return-on-investment provides a very basic form of measurement. You'll recall that we used this formula at the beginning of this chapter when discussing the hardware storeowner. Here's how the formula works:

$$ROI = \frac{\text{Income generated from investment—money spent on advertising}}{\text{Money spent on advertising campaign}}$$

Using the above example, the 11 responses our hardware salesman received from the $12.99 coupons yielded a return of $142.89. Subtract the cost of the ad, $32.00, and divide by $32.00. The result is 3.47, or 347%.

Monitoring Results On The Internet

Measuring advertising effectiveness on the Internet is easier than most other media. Information can be tracked in real time and in a precise way. Here are a few of the most pertinent metrics to track:

Clicks—the number of people who click on your banner
Sales/Conversions—the number of actual sales made from visitors to your website

In addition, Internet marketing gives you the chance to build up your "back end," meaning that, once you have captured the email address of site visitors, you can solicit them again. Since people often need to be exposed to a message multiple times before buying, Internet marketing allows for future sales.

A Final Word On Objectives

One of the biggest mistakes small businesses make is that they don't plan their marketing. Too often, marketing campaigns are put together on a whim. This hit-or-miss style of advertising often fails to generate the desired results and can waste a great deal of money. A consistent, well-planned campaign (that is carefully modified to adjust for changes in market conditions) will put your business on the track to success.

In addition, don't let unrealistic expectations kill your marketing campaign. Remember the hardware story from earlier in the chapter? Clearly, his expectations were unrealistic given the results.

Closing Exercise

Creating A Marketing Calendar

Take a moment to consider the next 12 months of your business. What are the busy times of year? Write out your marketing expectations for the next 52 weeks. Along with your marketing budget, this will be your tentative timeline and budget to work with. We'll take a look at how you will accomplish this in the upcoming chapters.

Example: Marketing Calendar

FEBRUARY 2007

SUN	MON	TUE	WED	THU	FRI	SAT
				1	2	3
4	5	6	7	8	9	10
11	12	13	14	15	16	17
18	19	20	21	22	23	24
25	26	27	28			

6

Selecting Media

When it comes to deciding where to advertise, one word typically describes the feeling most small business owners feel: Overwhelmed! And with good reason! From direct mail, phone directories, coupon mailers, and cable television to billboards, newspapers and the Internet (and that's the short list!), there's no shortage of options from which to choose. To add to the confusion, each of these mediums come with their own sales reps, each promising to deliver results that only their particular medium can reach. In truth, some can and will deliver the results you're looking for; others will not. More often, you will be using a combination of media (especially if you are a new business). The challenge for the small business owner is to choose which medium will reach your target market, so your advertising budget will be spent on something that will not fall short of expectations.

A Word About What Media "Works Best"

As a sales rep, I've often been asked which media works best: Newspapers or radio? Television or direct mail? Ultimately, there is not a "one size fits all" media vehicle (or advertising formula, for that matter) that is applicable to all businesses. I've had clients obtain great results at my former newspaper, where I sold advertising, only to have other clients get little or no response from the same paper. Truthfully, some media are better suited for some products and promotions than others. The trick is to find the right media for your business. An excellent place to start is by searching out what mediums are best suited for your particular business. This information can be gathered through industry associations, trade shows, and knowledge of local competition. **A word of warning: Just because your local competition advertises in one particular medium doesn't necessarily mean it is automatically the best medium for you.** However, it should provide you a reason to investigate further.

Case Study

As a local newspaper advertising rep, I was to create a dining page for our publication. A similar promotion had generated a great deal of revenue for our sister newspapers; they had brought in a great deal of revenue, and the advertisers reaped solid returns from the ads.

Unfortunately, a local, established competitor had been running a restaurant section in its newspaper for quite a while, and most of the local restaurants advertised in it. What's more, many had signed contracts and were locked into advertising in the paper. When I approached the restaurants, many managers scanned the paper and commented how there weren't any restaurants in my publications, so they didn't want to run.

Eventually, I managed to persuade a few of the restaurants to run in my newspaper, and they were so happy with the results, they included my paper in their advertising campaign. In addition to the results, the restaurants began to appreciate the fact that they didn't have to compete with so many other restaurants. After several months, I began to receive phone calls from restaurants that previously weren't interested in running with me. Now, they wanted to be included in my paper!

The lesson is simple: While it may be comforting to run with the competition, the name of the game is to reach your target market. This may or may not be in sync with what your competition is doing.

So, Where Do You Start?

Up to this point, we've been building the foundation for an advertising campaign. You've established an identity and mission, you've set up a marketing budget, and you've established objectives for your advertising campaign. Believe it or not, you've already done most of the leg work—the parameters you've already established will go a long way in helping you decide where to run your ad.

Let's recap what we've done so far:

1. Your target market: To whom are you marketing, men or women or both? Young? Old? What geographic location? High-end or low-end of the market?

2.   What is your budget?

3.   Is there a form of media in which your industry specializes?

Now, you're ready to step forward and decide where to advertise your business.

Media Selections

The world of media is expanding daily. Newspaper, magazine, radio, television, direct mail—the selection can be mind numbing. So, let's get started!

While all media may appear to be the same on the surface, the truth reveals subtle and not so subtle differences. For example, a radio station that plays love songs usually attracts a female audience, while an all-sports radio station attracts a predominantly male audience. Information regarding readers, listeners, or viewers of a particular form of media can be broken down to age, income, home ownership, type of car driven, zip code—just about any category imaginable.

Before you buy any media, ask for a media kit. A media kit is a packet that provides business owners with information about the medium's audience. This is your starting point. A media kit can be obtained at the media office, or you can call and have a sales rep deliver one to you. This may be a good opportunity to ask the sales rep about the media he or she represents.

Types Of Media

As previously mentioned, different media accomplish different things. Here is a summation of various media pros and cons:

Direct Mail

Considered a form of direct marketing, direct mail enjoys popularity among small businesses. (This goes along with Yellow Page and newspapers.) Direct mail allows advertisers to target a specific audience, often in a specific geographic area.

Buying Direct Mail

Direct mail takes on many forms. Franchises, like Advo and Money Mailer, sell direct mail opportunities, and other outfits, such as Chamber of Commerce, allow direct marketing opportunities as well. This form of advertising is often sold on a cost-per-thousand (CPM) basis. For example, if direct mail offers $6.50 per thousand, and you are looking to reach a population of 60,000, than it will cost $390.

Yellow Pages

By far, the most popular form of advertising for a small business is the yellow page directory. It is usually the mainstay of most small business advertising campaigns. Businesses that sell a product or service that people need in a pinch usually benefit the most from this form of advertising.

Typically, an ad that stands out has a better chance of being noticed—this is important if you are in an industry with heavy competition in the area. If you have a highly specialized business that caters to other businesses, you may also want to consider any business-to-business directories that are available. Yellow page advertising can be expensive, but many businesses find that it is worth it.

Buying Yellow Pages

Yellow pages can be purchased either by line or by space. Although directories tend to look alike, different directories have different policies regarding how space is purchased. Consult your local directory advertising rep for specifics.

Over the past several years, many different yellow page directories have sprouted up around the country. Consequently, it's not unusual to find that you have three or more of them for one area. Depending on the nature of your business, advertising in one or two directories should be sufficient. How do you decide which is best? Look to your target audience, and assess which directory would reach this target best. You may want to consider brand name and size as well as where the majority of your competition advertises.

Since most people now go online for information, you may also want to investigate any local online directories that are available.

Newspapers

Much has been written about the demise of the newspapers, but they are one of the most basic (and affordable) media vehicles around, second only to yellow pages in popularity amongst small businesses. In order to compete with direct mail and other specialized media, newspapers have developed specialty sections, such as sports, lifestyle, and business. With these specialty sections comes specific demographics. For example, the lifestyles section of a newspaper that contains recipes, travel information, and advice columns may have a high female readership, while the sports section appeals to a largely male audience. In addition, newspapers allow advertisers to customize ad size to fit any budget.

Buying Newspaper

While classified advertising is often sold on a cost-per-word basis, display advertising is typically sold on a CPM (Cost-Per-Thousand) basis, although sometimes it is sold in modular sizes. Computing ad cost on a CPM basis first requires figuring ad size, often in column inches, and multiplying it with a given rate. For example, if an ad is two column inches wide (the width of two columns in the newspaper) and 3 regular inches in height, the ad is said to be a size of 6 column inches. This number is then multiplied by a given dollar rate. If the rate for running one time is $8.50 a column inch, then the cost of the ad can be calculated by multiplying $8.50 x 6. The ad cost would be $51.00 to run one time.

Pricing structures of newspapers vary, so be sure to ask for a rate card from your sales representative.

Magazines

Magazines offer a way to use print to target a particular audience. According to the National Directory of Magazines (2005), during that year, there were no fewer than 18,267 magazines in the United States.* Go to any newsstand, and you can see hundreds of them at a glance.

Although competition from cable and the Internet have put a dent in magazine circulation, magazines offer a way to target an audience that can override the other media competition. One of the added benefits of magazines is the offering of special sections in the back of the magazine, which is specifically designed for direct response ads. Located under a special banner, magazine readers can shop for products and services usually related to the subject of the magazine.

---

*   National Directory of Magazines, 2005

Buying Magazine

Like newspapers, magazines typically charge on a cost-per-thousand basis. Magazines also sell ads in modular sizes (full page, half page, 2/3 page, etc.) Another similarity magazines have with newspapers is the classified section, which allows the advertiser to inexpensively reach a target audience.

Once you decide to advertise, the subject of position arises. The two most important factors regarding display advertising are visibility and proximity to editorial. Typically, the four most desirable display positions of the magazine are as follows:

1. Inside front cover

2. Outside back cover

3. Back cover

4. Opposite Table Of Contents

Usually, publishers like to lay out the magazine so readers must go through the entire book. That being said, having an ad in the front part of the book is usually the most desirable.

Many magazines publish regional editions. For a small business owner, this can be a cost-effective way of further targeting your message to your audience.

Radio

Although not as glamorous as other media, radio is one of the forms of media that is time tested as an efficient way to build awareness through repetition. What's more, radio offers an intimacy few media can match. Combined with other forms of targeted advertising, radio can bolster a campaign like no other media.

Buying Radio Time

Radio is a highly negotiable form of media, based largely on inventory. Consequently, radio salespeople try to convey a lack of availability in order to raise the rates they charge per ad spot. Like all other media, it's important to see if the radio format fits your audience. With all the formats available, you can usually find one that will reach your target consumers. Ask your advertising rep for demographic information pertaining to the radio station's target audience, as well its geographical reach.

Unlike print, which furnishes circulation numbers, radio measures listenership through Arbitron ratings, which convey what percentage of radio listeners tune in to a particular station during a particular time. These numbers break down according to age, gender, income, time of day, etc.

Cable

Cable television reaches over 2/3 of US homes via television. Less expensive than broadcast television, buying a spot on cable television can be a very effective way to advertise. With a vast array of specialized channels, the ever-growing selection of channels allows an advertiser to target an audience effectively. The ability to deliver sight, sound, motion, and emotion separates cable (and broadcast) television from other media.

Buying Cable

Cable television is sold in spot increments. Like other medium, frequency of delivering your message to your target audience is very important.

Famed advertising author Roy H. Williams has a common sense methodology for purchasing cable television. Williams suggests buying more frequently on one or a few networks and advertising on the same days, weeks, and months. The reason for this type of media buying is to expose the same people to your message over and over again, reinforcing the campaign. Buying in a broad rotation scattered across different channels at different times does not allow for this.

Interactive

More and more, the Internet is becoming a medium for small businesses. Local websites are registering increases in traffic, and even large search portals, such as Google, are looking for ways to get a piece of the local advertising dollar. According to the Internet Advertising Bureau, $12.5 billion was spent in 2005 on Internet advertising—a 30% increase in ad expenditure from 2004.

Buying Interactive

Advertising online is sold in a number of different ways. Banner advertising and ever-increasing emails are the dominant form of advertising. The first is our friend CPM, a model you should be familiar with at this juncture. Advertising is also sold on a cost-per-click and cost-per-acquisition format.

Additional Mediums

So far, we've covered mediums that are most likely to be used by small business. This is hardly an exhaustive list, however. Billboard, broadcast television, and other media are also available for small businesses. Usually, however, the capital needed to advertise using these mediums are usually out of reach for most small businesses. Nonetheless, you should investigate these or any media vehicle that will be the best way to reach your target audience.

A Word About Buying Advertising

It's not unusual for new business owners (and small business owners, in general) to be inundated by advertising salespeople and proposals. Like all occupations, advertising has its share of reputable professionals. Unfortunately, there are advertising reps that are less than respectable. Since salespeople are paid on commission, they often want to sign new businesses to long term advertising agreements immediately. One word of advice: Take your time! This is your business, and it's your money being spent on advertising. Don't commit to anything until you have a thorough understanding of what you are signing, and you feel comfortable with the rep. In the event you wish to advertise with a media outlet but don't like the rep, feel free to call the sales office and request another rep.

Ultimately, once you have an opportunity to measure the effectiveness of a medium, you can decide if you want to incorporate it into your advertising campaign. If you are pleased with the results, signing a contract for a longer-term deal is usually a good idea, since these agreements offer lower rates in exchange for added frequency. Remember to make sure these agreements fit into your advertising budget.

Develop A Working Relationship With Advertising Sales Reps

Just as you want a sales rep who is respectful, it's important to give respect in return. Being on time for meetings and respecting deadlines are elements of a fruitful relationship. If you want a reputable salesperson, it is important to be respectable and dependable yourself! What's more, a good relationship with an advertising rep can bear fruit that isn't always apparent on the surface. Advertising sales reps are usually well entrenched in the local business community and can be of great assistance in providing referrals for your business. Sales reps are also more likely to provide perks at no charge for those who make working together enjoyable. A sales rep can decide to give you a larger ad at no additional charge when the paper needs to fill up the extra space.

Case Study

As an advertising sales rep in Florida, I had the unique experience of living through Hurricane Francis—one of the biggest hurricanes to hit South Florida in years. Afterwards, there was damage in the form of destroyed buildings and no electricity. What's more, because there was no electricity, gas station pumps didn't work. For the days and weeks that followed, many of my customers found themselves in dire situations. Insurance claims had to be filed, FEMA grants applied for, and various others needs to be met.

In the days and weeks that followed, I checked in with my clients to see if they needed anything. Fortunately, as someone who was well connected with the community, I was able to answer questions they had about government assistance and insurance; in addition, I was able to connect them with other business owners and service providers they needed. It was the least I could do. Some of my clients lost their businesses; others were engaged in cleaning up and getting back to normal. In the weeks that followed, many of my clients thanked me for my help. The lesson? Good business is about fulfilling mutual needs. Developing a good relationship with your sales rep can benefit your business beyond advertising.

Frequency And Long Term Contracts

When purchasing advertising, chances are good that a sales rep will look to lock you up in a long-term deal. For the small business owner new to advertising, be careful about locking yourself into a long-term deal until you have a chance to measure the effectiveness of advertising. Seeing a new business owner lock up his or her limited advertising budget for a year-long contract for media that doesn't work is a common mistake—and one that should be avoided. Committing long-term to a medium that is ineffective isn't just a waste of marketing dollars; it hurts a business by bringing in fewer customers.

That being said, frequency is key to any good advertising campaign. Advertising only once in a newspaper, magazine, or any other medium is a waste of money. A target audience needs multiple exposures to even become aware of your business. When you consider that the average person is bombarded with hundreds of advertisements a day, the challenge becomes clear: repetition is mandatory.

Negotiating Media Buys

Unlike many other products and services, there is normally wiggle room when purchasing advertising. Depending on the economy and the media, you the buyer may have more negotiation room than you realize. Internet websites may have more inventory than they are selling, for example. If that is the case, the sales rep may have some room to negotiate. You may want to consult local or national business publications to get a feel for a particular form of media.

Media Comparisons

Direct Mail

Advantages

<u>Target-ability</u>: With direct mail, an advertiser can target potential advertisers by geographical area, product affinity, previous purchases, and potential interest based on accumulated or purchased databases.

<u>Reach</u>: The medium potentially can reach every household in the market, or at least every consumer the marketer wishes to target, usually through mail-merge options.

<u>Maintenance</u>: Direct mail can be helpful in building and reinforcing existing consumer relationships through personalized mailings.

<u>Tracking</u>: Marketers can track responses through coupon redemption and return-card/call-back options.

<u>Precision</u>: Direct mail allows an advertiser to convey highly detailed information about his or her product or service as well as deliver product samples for customers to try.

---

*   Media Facts, Radio Advertising Bureau, 2006

Disadvantages

<u>Low Response Rate</u>: Most direct mail marketers consider a response rate of 2 or 3 percent to be successful. This means that up to 98 percent of the people you target will reject or ignore your offer.

<u>Attention</u>: Much of the time, direct mail is thrown away unopened; when consumers actually read their direct mail, they tend to read mailings from advertisers they know and like.

<u>New Customers</u>: Direct mail is less effective in attracting new prospects than reinforcing existing customers. For any business whose future depends on expanding its customer base, this is a significant liability.

<u>Consumer Perception</u>: Most consumers refer to direct mail as "junk mail"—and they have an even lower opinion of the more cost—efficient, mail-merge packages that combine pieces from a number of different advertisers in one envelope.

<u>Outdated Mailing Lists</u>: Even among consumers who are not actively trying to have their names stricken from direct mail's rolls, there are many who move each year, making it difficult for direct mail companies to identify and maintain accurate databases.

<u>Declining Couponing</u>: Time crunched consumers are not clipping and redeeming coupons the way they once did, which reduces the impact and trackability of many direct marketing campaigns.*

<u>Growing Expense</u>: Direct mail costs are on the rise. Increases in postal rates, production charges, paper costs, and database fees have turned direct mail into one of the least cost-efficient of all media.

Yellow Pages

Advantages

<u>Widespread</u>: Almost every home and business in America (96.9%) has at least one copy of "the book."

<u>Usage</u>: Almost three out of five (58 percent) adults say they check the Yellow Pages for a phone number and/or address at least once a week, with 76 percent using the book monthly.

<u>Reference Tool</u>: The Yellow Pages serves as a directional reference for consumers who already have decided to purchase a product or service; of the consumers who use the Yellow Pages, 50 percent do not know from which store or business they will buy prior to looking in the directory.

<u>Emergency Reference</u>: Consumers often rely on the yellow pages during emergency situations.

<u>Target Consumers</u>: Ads primarily target consumers already interested in purchasing the product or service.

---

*   Media Facts, Radio Advertising Bureau, 2006

Disadvantages

<u>Limited Exposure</u>: Just over half of U.S. adults 18+ refer to the Yellow Pages in the average week. The other 42 percent will not see your ad.

<u>Minimal Consumer Awareness</u>: Since the Yellow Pages typically are consulted after the decision to buy has been made, top-of-mind awareness must be built in other ways. As products continue to proliferate and the retail market becomes saturated, you must create demand for your products before the buying decision has been made.

<u>Ad Clutter</u>: Your ad is lumped in with all the others for the same product, where shoppers can compare.

<u>Inconvenient</u>: Phone books tend to be big! They're bulky, hard to store, and not readily available to consumers outside the home or office. Their availability is limited to the locations where most purchases are made. How many pay phones have you seen with a complete phone book? (Indeed, as mobile phones continue to expand, how many people even use phone booths anymore?)

<u>Inflexible</u>: Most directories are published once a year, and advertising must be purchased well in advance of the publication date. You can't make corrections or changes resulting from dynamic business conditions or new opportunities.

<u>Too Many Books</u>: In many communities, there are several different directories all soliciting for your listing. Who reads them all? Who needs them all?

<u>Encroaching Competition from the Internet</u>: YellowPages-like services on the Internet are springing up; their supporters promise a more logical organization of data and the capability to update information more often.

Newspapers

Advantages

History: One of the oldest, most highly regarded media in the U.S. Among its loyal readers, it enjoys a high degree of familiarity, acceptance, credibility, and respect.

Visuals: The newspaper's combination of text and graphics, when used effectively, can create visual appeal that reinforces the messages of its advertising.

Mass Audience: Newspapers reach a relatively large mass audience throughout the market with a single exposure.

Ad Variety: The medium offers a variety of ad sizes that allows advertisers to meet their budgetary constraints.

In-Depth: Newspaper ads have the ability to communicate lengthy, complex, or detailed information and descriptions.

Ease of Tracking: It's relatively easy to track responses, primarily through couponing.

Lead Time: Advertisers can place orders and copy with a relatively short lead time.

Exposure: The reader controls the amount of exposure to a given ad. They can spend as much or as little time with an ad as they like.

---

*   Media Facts, Radio Advertising Bureau, 2006

Disadvantages

<u>Decreasing Penetration</u>: In most markets, circulation is less than 50 percent of all households (please ask for the RAB Newspaper Performance Report based on ABC data for your market).

<u>Ad Clutter, No Separation</u>: A typical daily newspaper is 60 to 62 percent advertising, not counting free-standing inserts. Your ad placed next to your competitors' can only be an advantage if your price is absolutely the lowest.

<u>Passive</u>: The paper provides information once consumers decide to buy, but it does not build brand awareness or create product demand. Newspaper advertising works mainly for comparing prices.

<u>Browsers, not Readers</u>: Most people don't read all the sections of the paper every day. Ads in a given section reach only those who read that section. Even the most-read section (Section 1) is seen by only about half the newspaper readers.

<u>Readers Don't See Ads</u>: On average, only 42 percent of readers will recall noting a full page ad (for specific ad-noting factors, see your market's RAB Newspaper Performance Report).

<u>Can't Target</u>: It's difficult to accommodate selective approaches that improve your cost efficiency and enhance frequency against clearly defined, high-potential customer segments.

<u>Couponing is Declining</u>: Despite increased coupon face value, redemption has been declining for years.

<u>New Competition from Outside</u>: One of newspaper's strongest ad categories (classifieds) is under attack both from Internet firms and savvy radio stations.

Alternative Newsweeklies

Advantages

<u>Distribution</u>: Weeklies usually are distributed free throughout the city.

<u>Pass-along Readership</u>: Because most are free, readers often leave them behind when they're done—to be picked up and read by someone else.

<u>Hip Image</u>: Many newsweeklies are targeted to hip, youngish readers who rarely look at daily newspapers. In particular, the local newsweekly is the source of choice for entertainment news among young demographics.

<u>"Budget" Print Ads</u>: An ad in a newsweekly offers many of the same characteristics as a newspaper ad—but at rates that are usually lower than those of the local newspaper.

<u>Accepting Ad Policies</u>: Ads for categories that may have difficulty finding a home in other media, such as liquor and tobacco advertising, are usually welcome here.

---

*   Media Facts, Radio Advertising Bureau, 2006

Disadvantages

Advertising Environment: The flip side of newsweeklies' open-handed ad acceptance policy is that the environment created by certain types of ads may not be suitable for mainstream businesses or products.

Limited Publication Schedule: The name "weekly" says it all. The majority of these publications are produced only once a week—and that may not be often enough to achieve sufficient message frequency.

Production Quality: Although some weeklies boast production values rivaling or even surpassing the local newspaper, many other are produced as cheaply as possible, resulting in a "cheap" look that may affect consumer perception concerning the quality of the product or service being promoted.

Narrow Appeal: The appeal of weeklies among younger demos may be fine if that's the target audience. However, advertisers seeking consumers who are older—and have more disposable income—may not find a good match here.

Inflexible: To meet the weekly's schedule, ads usually must be locked in as much as a week or more in advance, limiting an advertiser's ability to introduce copy changes.

Ad Clutter: Most weeklies rely completely on advertising revenue, so the typical issue is crammed with ads, often clustered together in groups. This practice can make it difficult for a given ad to stand out.

Magazines

Advantages

Readership: According to spring 2001 Simmons data, 89 percent of adults age 18 and older say they read one or more magazines.

Targetability: Specialty magazines allow advertisers to target consumers demographically, by product affinity, or by lifestyle.

Strong Visuals: Magazine ads can be highly creative and aesthetically appealing through the effective use of photography, graphics, color, and copy.

Portability: Magazines can be carried by consumers and read almost anywhere, at any time (in-car is one notable exception).

Advertorial: An in-depth advertising message can be created to appear more like editorial than an advertisement, although most magazines require such advertorials to be identified as advertising rather than editorial content.

Localizing: Regional/local editions, polywrap inserts, and local "vista" magazines offer local advertising opportunities.

---

*   Media Facts, Radio Advertising Bureau, 2006

Disadvantages

<u>Competition</u>: There are too many magazines—too many choices.

<u>Time</u>: The average person spends only 5 or 6 percent of his or her daily media time reading magazines.

<u>Clutter</u>: Magazines contain so much advertising that ad readership and recall is minimal. The typical magazine contains over 50 percent advertising, so there's little opportunity for consumers to absorb both the editorial content and advertising.

<u>Reach</u>: The proliferation in the number of magazines means audience fractionalization, and the most magazines actually miss most of their avowed target audiences. The average issue of Business Week reaches less than 3 percent of all professional manager adults, and Good Housekeeping misses more than 86 percent of adult women.

<u>Inflexible</u>: Because of lead time, advertising must be prepared long before publication dates, prohibiting advertisers from responding instantly to changing market conditions.

<u>Expensive</u>: Increased distribution and production costs have forced magazines' cost-per-thousand to almost double in the past 10 years.

<u>There are too many magazines</u>: Too many choices.

Cable Television

Advantages

<u>Growth Spurt</u>: Cable now reaches two thirds of all U.S. TV households and even more (80 percent vs. 49 percent in 1985) among households with an annual income over $50,000.

<u>Inexpensive</u>: Many advertisers consider cable to be "discount television." Cable offers some of the same benefits (e.g., motion, visuals, sound) as broadcast television but at considerably cheaper rates.

<u>Targetable</u>: Cable can subdivide its audience into much more easily targeted segments than over-the-air TV can. More than half (60 percent) of viewers have 54 or more choices. Such an array of choices allows advertisers to target specific consumer groups according to their programs of interest.

<u>Consumer Appreciation</u>: Most consumers like the cable they pay to receive. In 2000, Americans spent an estimated $39 billion subscribing to cable and ancillary services, such as telephone and Internet access.

<u>Summer Season</u>: When the broadcast networks' shows go on hiatus in the summertime, their reruns yield pride of place to cable networks' original programming.

---

*   Media Facts, Radio Advertising Bureau, 2006

Disadvantages

<u>Small Audiences</u>: Because cable TV gives the viewers so many channels to choose from, cable audiences are considerably smaller than those of broadcast TV. During prime time, even the top cable networks rarely exceed 3 percent penetration among TV households. Furthermore, competition from satellite TV has forced operators to offer digital cable service, which means more options/fragmented audiences.

<u>Inaccurate Local Numbers</u>: As many of 12 percent of U.S. households get their programming from alternative delivery systems (ADS) such as satellite TV—and the percentage is much higher in many major markets. Because ADS subscribers cannot receive local commercials on national cable programming, any advertiser who relies on local-market Nielson books to get a handle on cable delivery in his or her DMA must deduct the ADS percentage of the audience, or they get less than they pay for.

<u>Limited Commercial Impact</u>: Cable is still locked out of a third of U.S. homes, and penetration is unlikely to increase too much beyond present levels. Cable (basic+premium) accounts for just 39 percent of all U.S. household TV set usage.

<u>Ad Clutter</u>: It's even worse than over-the-air television. While network TV typically carries a 24-unit spot load every hour, cable often carries as many as 28 units per hour—17 percent more—making ads much more annoying and, therefore, more susceptible to zipping, zapping, and time-shifting.

<u>Quality</u>: Local advertisers' spots often are placed cheek-by-jowl with national ads. As a result, they are forced to choose between spending an ever-increasing portion of their budgets in an attempt to achieve comparable quality or accepting the disparity in production values and airing ads that look cheap by comparison.

Internet

Advantages

<u>Direct Response</u>: With the Internet, you can reach highly educated and affluent consumers who are able to purchase your products or services with the click of a mouse.

<u>Interactivity</u>: The Internet allows your customers to communicate directly with you; they can tell you what they like and don't like, what they want, and what they will buy.

<u>Tracking</u>: Internet technology allows you to measure exactly how many people see your message … and how they respond.

<u>Immediacy</u>: Thanks to online commerce, your message can reach consumers just before they buy online … and offer detailed information to shape the buying decision.

<u>Flexible</u>: The Internet allows you to change your message frequently; in fact, Internet experts suggest that you must continually change your offerings to keep them fresh.

<u>New and Exciting</u>: As more and more consumers buy their first computer or finally get around to acquiring an Internet connection, there is a steady influx of consumers experiencing the Web for the first time. This sense of novelty and wonder will persist for some time before Web surfing becomes an experience to be taken for granted.

*   Media Facts, Radio Advertising Bureau, 2006

Disadvantages

<u>Perception</u>: Advertising is becoming more accepted on the Internet. However, the flip side of increased acceptance is decreased awareness. Many Internet users simply tune out ads or even block them with software designed for that purpose.

<u>Consumer Concerns</u>: In theory, e-commerce is safe, simple, and easy. However, despite evidence of the security of online transactions, publicized reports of credit-card theft on the Net have made many consumers hesitant to use their credit card number online.

<u>Time</u>: Although the installed base of high-speed Internet technology is growing, a significant base of users still access the Web using modem speeds of 56 kbps or slower. Hardware bottlenecks make navigating the Net a slow, tedious process for them. Many users, turned off by the time it takes to view graphic-heavy pages, move on quickly when they don't think the site is worth the wait.

<u>Infrastructure Problems</u>: The 2000 online holiday shopping season taught e-tailers some bitter lessons. As consumers flood the Internet looking to shop and buy, sites that don't sufficiently prepare for the onslaught will be plagued by painfully slow-loading times or outright crashes. Moreover, e-tailers are very dependent on timely shipping, a possible weak link that could break down just when it's needed the most. Loss of online visitors means your advertising will be less effective.

Outdoor

Advantages

<u>Brevity</u>: Outdoor advertising is effective for conveying brief messages and simple concepts.

<u>Building Word of Mouth</u>: Billboards can generate curiosity in "teaser" campaigns.

<u>Low Cost: Outdoors cost-per-thousand is significantly lower than that of any other advertising medium</u>—In some cases by a factor of 10 or even 20.

<u>Attention Grabbing</u>: The combination of size, color, and illumination attracts attention.

<u>Full-Time Audience</u>: Outdoor's message can appear year-round. For additional fees, outdoor advertisers can purchase evening lighting—or, in some cases, even 24-hour illumination.

<u>Directional</u>: Billboards can be used as directionals, pointing out the locations of a given business.

<u>Strategic Placement</u>: Billboards can be placed in high-traffic areas or other strategic locations, while transit signs can be affixed to the backs and sides of buses, in bus stops, and in rail stations.

---

*   Media Facts, Radio Advertising Bureau, 2006

Disadvantages

Brevity: The very nature of outdoor advertising demands that the commercial message be brief and relatively simple. Therefore, it is difficult to communicate product details, competitive advantages, and specific consumer benefits.

Limited Availability: Prime outdoor locations (in high-traffic areas) often are controlled by large, long-term advertisers. Construction of new billboards is restricted by costs, space availability, rigid municipal codes, and environmental regulations.

Lack of Effective Measuring Tools: Unlike other advertising media, outdoor advertising has no truly reliable method to measure its effectiveness. A few studies have been done, but they mostly apply to limited geographical areas and employ widely—varying methodologies.

Low Recall: Commuters behind the wheel and other potential customers are exposed very briefly to outdoor messages, minimizing message retention. Such adverse conditions, such as heavy traffic or bad weather, also can limit message impact and recall.

Ugly Image: Because of growing environmental concerns, many communities have eliminated, reduced, or limited the volume and placement of outdoor advertising.

Inflexible: Once a message is up, it generally stays up through the duration of the contract, even if the advertisers' needs have changed. Ads must be purchased an average of 28 days prior to showing in order to allow time for production and placement, which prohibits any corrections or additions that may result from changing business conditions.

Broadcast TV

Advantages

<u>Widespread</u>: Over-the-air television reaches virtually all Americans. Ninety-eight percent of U.S. households have at least one TV.

<u>Time Spent</u>: People spend a lot of time with their television sets. On average, U.S. viewers watch television almost 18 hours a week. Almost six hours of this is devoted to the major broadcast networks.

<u>Way of Life</u>: Baby Boomers (34- to 50-years-old) and Generation Xers (18-to-33-year-olds) grew up with TV … and the medium continues to attract new, young audiences.

<u>Mass Exposure</u>: Some television programs can reach large mass audiences with a single exposure.

<u>Visual Appeal</u>: TV has the ability to grab attention and create appeal through the combination of pictures, sound, and motion.

---

*   Media Facts, Radio Advertising Bureau, 2006

Disadvantages

<u>Audience Share is Decreasing</u>: Television's network prime time audience has decreased dramatically, from 90 percent in 1980 (ABC, CBS, NBC) to just 36 percent (ABC, CBS, NBC) in 2000. The last increase—just one rating point, and for only one year—occurred in the 1993-94 season and was the only positive blip in a 20-year downward spiral.

<u>VCR/DVD Use Decreases Viewership</u>: As VCR and DVD player uses increase, the impact of TV commercials decreases. Most homes (85 percent) have at least one VCR, and DVD household penetration in the U.S. has reached the one-third mark in just a few short years.

<u>Channel Surfing</u>: When a commercial comes on, many viewers go surfing. They jump from channel to channel to avoid the commercials. Personal video record-ers make it even easier to dodge the ads, giving the consumers the power to skip over commercials even in live broadcasts.

<u>Viewing Decreases as Income Increases</u>: U.S. adults whose household incomes are in the top third are statistically more likely to be light TV viewers.

<u>Skyrocketing Production Costs</u>: A typical, 30-second, national commercial can cost hundreds of thousands of dollars to produce.

<u>Restricted Viewing</u>: Almost all television viewing takes place at home, making it extremely unlikely that television advertising will influence consumers close to the point of purchase.

Point-Of-Purchase

Advantages

Placement: P-O-P advertising can be placed almost anywhere in stores—next to merchandise, on shopping bags, at the checkout counter, even suspended from the ceiling or laminated into floor tiles.

Targeted: P-O-P is most effective when it is positioned to reach a clearly-defined consumer target at the closest time of purchase.

Effective: Place-based advertising directly affects sales, brand switching, portfolio purchasing, and multi-unit sales.

Influential: P-O-P advertising gives retailers the opportunity to influence consumers in a competitive environment.

Incremental Sales: P-O-P advertising can persuade shoppers to purchase additional quantities of a product or to buy related products that are merchandised together.

---

*   Media Facts, Radio Advertising Bureau, 2006

Disadvantages

<u>Limited Reach</u>: By definition, place-based advertising only reaches that small group of consumers walking past displays, waiting at the checkout counter, or carrying their bags to the car. Moreover, studies show P-O-P marketing works best when geared towards younger, single, less-affluent shoppers.

<u>Product-Oriented</u>: Place-based advertising influences what products consumers may buy, but not where they will buy them. Though often effective for improving product sales, placed-based media inherently are limited in their ability to attract new customers, build traffic, and improve market awareness for retail advertisers.

<u>Consumer Perception</u>: Many consumers report that in-store TV monitors, electronic signs, and in-store broadcasting have little impact on them as they shop (they also claim that these devices blend into the environment).

<u>Shoppers</u>: Only about 20 percent of supermarket shoppers browse the aisles in drugstores or discount stores; the rest completely miss promos, displays, or special signage in these stores.

<u>Limited Targeting</u>: Despite its key placement, general-reach, place-based advertising (such as in store television) delivers limited results and can be prohibitively expensive.

Radio

Advantages

<u>Personal, the Theatre of the Mind</u>: Even though radio is only a sound medium, it is a very personal medium. Radio can involve and excite people's imaginations with scenes and stories that would be impossible to put in a television commercial. Radio is second only to television in its ability to emotionally involve people.

<u>Frequency and Reach</u>: Radio is an inexpensive medium, and frequency can be purchased efficiently. Radio is also even more ubiquitous than television. Because of radio's extensive penetration, it can extend past the reach of any other medium.

<u>Low Production Costs, Fast Closing</u>: Lowest production costs of all media. Some of the most effective commercials cost nothing and are read by on-air personalities. Commercial copy can be added or changed on a same-day basis, if necessary.

<u>Efficient</u>: In terms of CPM's, radio is the lowest medium, except outdoors. Radio offers both reach and frequency efficiently.

<u>Imagery Transfer</u>: Studies show that by airing the studio portion of a well-crafted television commercial, radio can stimulate the mind to recreate the visual image originally placed there by television, which costs a lot less than it does on a television screen.

<u>Competitive Separation</u>: Radio provides more separation than newspapers and yellow pages.

<u>Intrusive</u>: Not as intrusive as television, but more intrusive than print or outdoor.

<u>Targetability</u>: Similar to magazines in ability to target a wide variety of age, interest, lifestyle, and gender groups. Especially effective at touching hard-to-reach teens, minorities, and ethnic groups.

<u>Portable</u>: Radio is everywhere. There is more radio listening in cars than there is at home. You cannot read a newspaper or magazine, watch cable or broadcast television, or surf the Internet while driving a car, but you can listen to radio and look at billboards—an excellent combination of media.

---

*   Media Facts, Radio Advertising Bureau, 2003

Disadvantages

<u>Sound Only</u>: You cannot show or demonstrate a product or its package and label on radio. Although the human voice is personal and warm, many advertisers believe they need a picture of their store, product, or themselves to sell their product.

<u>Increased Clutter</u>: Though not as cluttered as television, in the last several years radio has become more cluttered with not only more commercials in an hour but also more commercials appearing in a single commercial break, which limits a commercial's impact.

<u>Linear Access</u>: Unlike print, listeners cannot go back or forward to hear a commercial again; when it is gone, it is gone. Commercials have no shelf life.

<u>Fragmentation</u>: In some markets, there are more than 60 radio signals competing for listener attention and advertiser money. Even though radio as a medium can deliver reach, in many markets, to match the reach of a newspaper or a television station, 10 or 20 radio stations have to be purchased, making it difficult to buy.

7

Adding Public Relations to Your Marketing Campaign

In today's media-saturated world, it's become increasingly difficult for small business owners to use advertising to cut through the noise. What's more, the general public has become increasingly distrustful of advertising. As a result, public relations has become an effective way of not only reinforcing an existing marketing campaign, but an effective way of building public trust.

For the purposes of the small business owner, public relations is a way of having your business mentioned through non-advertising means. Having a reporter write a feature about your business, for example, is an example of PR. Having your company mentioned in an industry newsletter or featured on the television news or radio is another example. Contributions to local organizations, such as sponsoring a local little league team or local non-profit fundraiser, will also work.

Public Relations and Advertising

In a day and age where the public tends to be suspicious of advertising, appearing in a news story lends credibility that is not found in advertising. People tend to believe what they read, and an article that appears about a business gives that business the kind of credibility that is worth more than any advertisement (assuming it's positive!).

A Quick Primer

Media outlets—from newspapers to magazines and radio to local television news—have one thing in common: content. They have to provide new and interesting news and human interest articles on a regular basis. It is a challenge for publishers and broadcasters to hold the attention of their subscribing, listening and viewing audience through the provision of continually fresh content on a daily basis.

Unlike advertising, there is no guarantee that you will receive publicity even after your business is introduced. Coverage depends on many factors, including the amount of news covered. Whether editors and reporters see events surrounding your business as newsworthy depends on many things.

Word of Warning: Even though you may advertise with a media outlet, that does not mean they will provide free publicity. While some media publications do offer "advertorials," or free publicity to advertisers, many hard news outlets do not. Indeed, the editorial staff and advertising staff rarely interact, and for good reason: news outlets need to maintain the appearance of impartiality. Consequently, they bend over backwards to keep both separate.

How Do You Get Publicity?

There are a number of ways a small business owner can receive free media coverage. Here are a few examples:

1. *Introduce yourself to local editors:* If you have a tech company, for example, you may want to introduce yourself to the reporter for the tech column in the local paper, as well as the business manager. Offering to be a resource for them when writing a story is a good way to become part of their Rolodex.

2. *Notify media outlets when something out of the ordinary happens to your business:* A grand opening, landing a special account, sponsoring an event, and making a donation to a local charity or civic organization are good reasons to notify media.

3. *Familiarize yourself with media:* Become familiar with the writing topics and styles of the reporters and editors of media outlets. More importantly, step out of your business owner role and become a reader. What do you find interesting to read? Would a story idea you propose really be of interest to an editor, or is it simply interesting to you? Be selective with what you choose to submit.

Case Study

Years ago, I worked for a real estate marketing firm that specialized in marketing high-end real estate. The firm employed cutting edge marketing and advertising techniques, and it was quite successful in reaching high-end clientele.

As a public relations consultant, it was my job to build the public relations arm of the business. One of my clients, who was in the process of building high-end condominiums, demanded to know why a competitor was always in the newspaper while he wasn't.

After some research, it was easy to see why. My client's competitor was active in hosting fund raising events for local community charities and organizations at no charge. What made this newsworthy was that the charities could never afford to hold these events if they had to pay for them. This was a model of the kind of business the community, which was looking to change its image, embraced. Consequently, local media were anxious to publicize these "feel good" stories.

Unfortunately, our client, who had business interests throughout the state, saw no value in working with the community from which he was making a living. His answer to generate public relations was to throw a high-end gala and invite the notables of the town—an idea he eventually gave up. Consequently, the amount of publicity he garnered in the local media was quite small. To the local editors and reporters, he was just another builder looking to make a quick buck in the real estate market.

A Final Word

Like advertising, public relations require a consistent effort. Maintaining relationships with editors and producers increases the likelihood that an editor will publicize your business. Also, publicizing events or circumstances that are newsworthy will increase your chances for write-ups as well.

8

Other Forms Of Marketing

Although advertising and public relations comprise the bulk of most marketing campaigns, they aren't the only ways to drum up sales. Here's a list of other forms of marketing that you may want to consider:

Brochures—Having a printed brochure outlining what your business does and offers along with contact information can be helpful as leave behinds, inquiries for information and trade shows.

Flyers—Handouts can be a very effective way to get the word out at events or high traffic areas. In addition, you can post them in high traffic areas frequented by your target market.

Events—Renting a booth at trade shows or conventions can help gain industry recognition. It also allows you to meet other vendors and learn valuable industry information.

Sponsorships—Sponsoring a trade show or even local sports teams can help spread the word. Local community sponsorships help show that you are an integral part of the community, even if you're a new business.

Chambers of Commerce/Industry Events—Pressing the flesh and networking with other business owners can lead to strategic alliances that help increase business.

Business Cards—Always have some on hand—you never know when a business opportunity will arise!

Sales—Depending on your business, hiring a sales staff may be necessary to spread the word and to make sales.

An Additional Word Regarding Internet Marketing

Although we already covered Internet advertising in Chapter 6, an additional word is needed regarding the Internet.

While many see the Internet as the domain of large companies looking for a national or international reach, the fact of the matter is the Internet is becoming more local all the time. Nowadays people are turning to the Internet to find everything from a local pizza place to a local electrician. Advertising on local search directories can be cost effective and generate solid business. Very soon, online searches will be as commonplace as e-mails.

The Internet also offers a number of ways to advertise your business. Blogs, website optimization, pay-per-click campaigns, e-mail campaigns—all can be very effective. If you think online marketing will comprise a large role in your marketing plan, some additional research is in order. Fortunately, there is lot's of information on the subject for beginners. Go to any local bookstore (or better yet, conduct an online search!) and take a look at books and magazines that specialize in small business advertising. Since the Internet is in a constant state of change, make sure you have the most up-to-date information available. A website or search engine that was tops 6 months ago may not be so today.

Depending on your understanding of online marketing, you may want to contact local companies that specialize in Internet marketing programs for small business. In addition to designing and hosting sites, many of these companies offer web optimization services as well.

If you think online advertising and PR would benefit your company, take a look at our Recommended Reading section at the end of this book.

9

Putting It All Together

At this point, it may be helpful to review what we've covered. The following diagram is a quick recap:

Multiple Marketing Channels

The term *multiple marketing channels* refers to the use of more than one form of marketing taking place simultaneously. For example, suppose the following events occurred in a one week period:

- An article on your business appears in the local newspaper

- A direct mail coupon for your business drops

- You implement an online advertising campaign on a local website

This form of marketing is the most effective of all. Why? Because repetition is key in advertising. **When your marketing message is presented through different forms of media, the impact is powerful. Not only is your message reinforced in the mind of the consumer, but you will have a higher degree of success connecting to your target market through multiple channels than through one single channel.**

Exercise

Back in Chapter 5, I asked you to put together a tentative 12 month marketing calendar based on your marketing budget. Now it's time to revisit that calendar and plug in the various marketing methods outlined in this book. For example, if you own a chocolate store, you may want to advertise in the local paper, the online town directory, and submit a press release to the local media presenting a unique story idea involving your business two weeks leading up to Valentine's Day.

Hopefully, you have some idea of what marketing vehicles you want to use based on research or experience. Even if you are set on your marketing, however, you will want to do some experimentation from time to time. As we mentioned before, the marketing world is always changing. New alternatives are always coming along, and you may find that a form of media that you may not have considered in the past may be a good fit for you today.

10

Common Mistakes

Over the years, I've had the opportunity to work with many small businesses. Routinely, I've seen many of these businesses make the same mistakes. Below you will find a list of the top mistakes. Read them, learn from them, and avoid them!

1. *Advertising one time:* Too many small business owners not familiar with advertising think they can judge the effectiveness of the medium after just running the advertisement one time. When I tell clients that running an ad frequently is the only way the ad can be truly effective, some view this suggestion as a slick sales technique to pry them away from their money.

    By now, you should know that frequency is the name of the game in advertising, and that a one-time run is really a waste of money. Of course, when a business owner runs an ad one time and receives few responses, it tends to reinforce his or her notion that "Advertising doesn't work" or "Your (fill in the media) doesn't work."

2. *Signing a long term contract before a medium has proven itself:* On the other side of the coin, I have met with business owners who wanted to advertise, but had money already contracted to a media outlet that was running ineffective ads. The reason? Some unsavory advertising rep played on their naivete by signing them up. This tied up their limited dollars and prevented them from growing their business.

3. *Irrational expectations:* Because of their limited understanding of advertising, some business owners expect their business to increase by 50% after two weeks of advertising. While this can happen (particularly with a new business), it's not a realistic expectation. In addition, factors—such as time of year, economic circumstances, severe competition, and even the weather—can play a role in the return from advertising. Having reasonable expectations is important.

4. *Letting your love for your business cloud your judgement:* Some of the worst advertising campaigns often come from business owners who are unable to step away and see how their business fits into the big picture. Ad copy that is self-serving only ends up serving the person who created it and has no impact on attracting new business. Putting yourself in the shoes of your customers is important.

5. *Cutting back on advertising during down cycles:* When the economy slows down, one of the first areas business owners wish to cut back on is advertising. This is a bad move. Truthfully, a business—especially a new business—should not surrender market share to those who do continue to advertise, which is what happens. In addition, studies routinely show that when companies drastically reduce advertising during down cycles, they not only lose clients during that time, but they are also the slowest to rebound when the economy picks up.

6. *The "I've been here for years—everyone knows I'm here" mentality:* In today's mobile society, people move all the time, which means that the people who know where you are located will someday move out, and new people who don't know your business move in—and have no idea who you are and where you are located. What's more, new businesses enter the marketplace daily. In today's economy, very few businesses have the luxury of sitting back and doing nothing to promote their business.

7. *Word of mouth:* By far, this is the most misunderstood concept as it relates to marketing. The fact is, unless you offer something in a market that is tremendously underserved and has a high demand for your product or service, the chances of pure word-of-mouth advertising carrying business to you is slim. For truly original products or services, this may hold true-but it's rare.

    Now, that doesn't mean that word of mouth has no effect. If you provide excellent service or a product that is truly unique, word of mouth will help you big time—nothing beats a personal referral! Unfortunately, word of mouth travels even faster when someone has a bad experience, which is something you obviously want to avoid!

8. *Expecting free publicity in a newspaper because you advertise in it:* As we covered earlier, most hard news publications do not connect advertising and editorial in order to maintain editorial integrity. Some publications do offer this and often mention this during the sales process. Newspapers and other

media offer an opportunity for you to communicate with their audience for a fee. Beyond this, there is no obligation.

9. *Expecting advertising to make-up for poor business practices:* Regardless of how much advertising you do, nothing can compensate for poor service, unreliability, shoddy workmanship, or overpriced goods or services. Once again, business owners often times lack the ability to look objectively at their business. Many consider their business to be great, when in truth, they are not. **Part of being successful in business is having the proper perspective.**

10. *Poor offer/poor copywriting:* Publishing a coupon promising 10% off any item won't lure many people to your business, unless the average price tag of your product or service runs in the hundreds or thousands of dollars. Remember that your offer has to motivate people to sample your business.

Likewise, poor copywriting will cost you potential business. If you are unsure of what to say or how to say it in an ad, consult with your account representative and ask their opinion. Because they typically work on commission, it's in their interest to share their expertise to insure your campaign is a success. If they don't, you may want to consult some copywriting books (we recommend a few at the end of this book) or hire an advertising consultant.

11

Creating Advertising Copy That Sells

When you decide to market your business, it's time to choose what it is you want to communicate. Next to purchasing your advertising, this is the one element of advertising that strikes fear in the hearts of most small business owners!

But, I bring you good news! You don't have to go it alone! In addition to selling advertising, the advertising sales reps usually have expertise in the areas of communications and target audience interest. From print to radio to cable television, media companies have staff available to put together spec ads for you; in addition, they also have experienced professional production staff members whose job involves putting together a campaign for you. As for visual element, advertising reps offer this as a free part of the advertising they are selling.

Nonetheless, even if you are working with advertising professionals, being able to *communicate* why your target market should select your product or service from other businesses is crucial. In addition, being able to communicate your business to others through various other marketing venues (brochures, chamber of commerce directories, etc.) is critical as well. Besides, after all is said and done, who knows your business better than you?

Where To Start

Remember the mission statement we worked on in Chapter Two? Similar to that, we will be using your answers to these questions to forge ahead in creating ad copy that sells.

Your Business Brand

Earlier in the book, you also put together a business brand. Keep the answer to these questions close at hand when beginning the copywriting process. As you attempt to communicate your business, always keep your target market in mind.

What Makes A Good Ad?

The staple of a good ad is fairly simple: At the very least, the ad should be aesthetically appealing, have a headline, make an emotional or logical appeal, and include a call to action. Sound frightening? Relax. Creating an ad that meets these criteria is simpler than you think.

Before you get started, take note of the ads you see in the newspaper, magazines, on the radio, television—and even in direct mail. Although each of these mediums has its own writing style, you can begin to see that ads within a medium tend to take on a consistent form. What's more, they tend to use similar vocabulary. Here's a sample of some of the common words and phrases:

Free	Introducing
Proven	Announcing
New	Last chance
Easy	Latest
Unique	Guaranteed results[*]

In addition, a good ad has an aesthetic appeal. It looks good. The logo graphic compliments the business brand, and the ad isn't too cluttered.

Exercise
Go through a newspaper and look at the ads. What words and phrases are most commonly used? What words or phrases do you think are effective? Write them down.

---

[*]   *Write Great Ads* by Erica Levy Klein

Putting It All Together

Even if you don't think of yourself as "creative," you can still write effective copy. And even if you don't plan on writing ad copy, you should be familiar with the standard body of an ad.

Excercises

The following are questions from Erica Levy Klein's book *Write Great Ads*. Carefully think about each question before writing a response:

1. Describe your product or service.

2. How will the customer benefit from purchasing your product or service?

3. What makes it different from the competition?

4. Does your product or service exude proof of the benefits?

5. What special offer are you proposing to motivate the prospective customer to act now?

6. What are any additional benefits (accepting credit cards, money back guarantee, etc.)?

7. Write a sentence that describes what your business does and who, specifically, benefits from it. This will function as your tagline.

Standard Rule Of Advertising Copy

The body of a good advertisement is simple in its makeup. Basically, it consists of the following:

Visual Appeal
Headline
Benefits
Supportive Claims
Call To Action

David Ogilvy, the famed advertising guru who literally wrote the book on advertising with the classic, *Ogilvy on Advertising,* was ahead of his time in realizing that the amount of attention consumers spend actually looking at an ad is short. Consequently, an ad has to do a lot of work in a very short period of time. **It's also important to keep your message direct and simple.**

Further Assistance

Copywriting is not a "one size fits all" activity. In fact, while the basics of good advertising as outlined above are common to most ads, the writing style and techniques of creating an effective ad vary from medium to medium. For example, copywriting for a newspaper ad is different than copywriting for a radio spot. Likewise, television commercial copywriting is different than an Internet banner. Describing what goes into an ad in every different genre of media would be a book unto itself.

There are numerous books on the subject of copywriting, but I recommend *Write Great Ads* by Erica Levy Klein. It's a simple, short, easy-to-read book with simple and easy exercises for most media.

A Final Word

Creating effective advertising is part art, part science. While it seems everyone has heard of a business pulling an outrageous publicity stunt, most successful small business advertising combines proven formulas with an intimate knowledge of the target audience. Objectively placing yourself in the shoes of your target audience is often times difficult for small business owners. They have invested so much of themselves in their business that they have a tough time being objective.

Yet, it is important to cast a critical eye at your own creation and see it through the eyes of your prospective clients.

12

Hiring an Advertising Agency

For some small businesses, and new businesses in particular, the thought of advertising (and putting together marketing materials, for that matter) can be overwhelming. Between financing the businesses, buying equipment or inventory, and servicing clients, many business owners, while they understand the need to advertise in today's competitive environment, simply don't feel they have the time or energy to invest in creating and maintaining an advertising campaign.

If you fit into this category, you may want to consider using an advertising agency. Before you move in this direction, however, there are some questions you should ask in order to make the right decision.

Things to Know Before You Make That First Inquiry

Before hiring an advertising agency, there are several steps the small business owner should take.

1. *Decide what you want from an advertising agency:* Do you want help creating direct mail copy, or someone to oversee the entire direct mail process? Do you need someone to create ads and copy for local newspapers? Do you desire help coordinating various advertising campaigns (print and direct mail, for example)? Knowing exactly what function you want the advertising agency to perform must be your first step in determining if an agency is right for your business. In today's world of specialization, you may only require the assistance of a freelance advertising copywriter, graphic artist or a direct marketing mail house instead of an advertising agency.

2. *Keep your advertising budget in mind:* Small advertising agencies can bill by the hour, by a retainer fee, or charge a percentage of the media buy (usually, 15%).

3. *Expectations:* Have a solid expectation of your Return-On-Investment (ROI). Since you have already worked on much of this already, you should have these numbers immediately at your fingertips.

Hiring an Advertising Agency

Hiring an advertising agency is one of the more unique experiences in business. Somewhere between hiring a vendor and bringing on a partner (hypothetically speaking!), the relationship between a small business owner and an advertising agency must be close. In order to understand what needs to be done, the agency needs to know the vision and target market for your business. What's more, they need to understand the culture of your business in order to communicate and publicize your business effectively. Here's a quick checklist of things to keep in mind when hiring:

1. *Referrals:* Ask the agency to provide a list of current clients (many agencies have this posted on their websites). Then, contact them and ask if they like working with the agency. If you know of another small business owner who uses an advertising agency, you may want to ask them. You may also want to contact your local chamber of commerce or a local chapter of the professional association representing your profession. Approaching someone whose work you are familiar with, or who specializes in advertising for businesses your size, is essential.

2. *Meet with the person who will be working on your campaign:* If you are working with a small agency, more than likely the person you speak with at the agency will be handling your account. Sometimes, however, an account executive who is unfamiliar to you may be assigned to work on your account, with the agency owner or chief officer overseeing them. Since you will be working with the account executive on a day-to-day basis, you should meet and interview him or her first. Ask who will be working with you and request to meet with the individual assigned to your business.

3. *Make sure you are on the same page:* Does the agency listen and ask questions to learn about your business? Do you feel comfortable working with the agency and the person you will be working with on a daily basis? An essential element of a successful campaign is to have a good working relationship with the agency.

4. *Does the agency work on the campaign of a competitor:* An agency working for a competitor, especially a larger competitor that does a great deal of advertising, may not be right for you. In addition to a conflict of interest, the agency will more than likely not give you the attention you are paying for or deserve.

5. *What you need from the agency, specifically:* Advertising agencies are famous for putting on very persuasive presentations. After all, they are in the image business! However, an agency may try to sell you services you don't need, which will add increases to the pricetag. While you want to be open to suggestions (remember, the reason you're looking to hire someone to assist you with your advertising campaign is to benefit from their expertise!), don't be afraid to ask questions if a proposal doesn't sound right to you.

6. *Does the agency have experience in the area of advertising you're inquiring about?* : If you need help with print advertising, the chances of a firm that specializes in interactive marketing providing you with the help you need is slim. Make sure the agency with whom you are speaking is qualified.

Hiring a Consultant

Advertising agencies make their money by selling their expertise. In effect, they are in the business of making money, plain and simple. The culture of advertising can be fast and loose, and there are some unscrupulous agencies that look to take advantage of new, small business owners whom they may see as naïve. They also may feel that the business owner has placed them under the gun to generate unrealistic profits immediately. Hiring a marketing consultant can help you navigate through the landscape of advertising agencies.

Do You Really Need an Advertising Agency?

Often times, small business owners have inexpensive, or in some cases, free resources at their disposal that never dawned on them. As stated earlier, media outlets provide services, like copywriting and graphics, for free to their clients. Likewise, direct mail businesses offer copywriting services and graphic services for a small fee (and sometimes free) as part of their services. The same holds true for printing services. Printing shops can help you with graphics assistance as well.

Time Management and Effective Advertising Campaigns

Businesses need customers to survive, and advertising is the means by which a business communicates with potential customers. The most successful new and small businesses know this and make advertising a regular part of their business routine. After all, no one knows your business like you!

Regardless of whether or not you decide to hire an advertising agency or marketing consultant, one thing is certain: You need to be as disciplined about managing your advertising as you are with financial statements and other critical business functions. Those that take advertising seriously (and, consequently, customer retention and customer acquisition) do better than their competition.

Final Thoughts

Congratulations! After reading this book and completing the exercises provided, you've taken a very important step in insuring that your business will earn the profits you've imagined.

As we've mentioned many times, discipline and consistency are critical ingredients when putting together an effective marketing campaign. It's important to take stock of marketing results and market conditions, so you can adjust your strategies accordingly. If you are interested in learning more about advertising your business, take a look at our *Recommended Reading* section.

Today's business climate is as difficult as ever, and the winners in this business world are those establishments that know how to communicate with their target market. By taking a disciplined, proactive approach, you are ready to leap to the head of your business field.

Happy Earnings!

Recommended Reading

Positioning: The Battle For Your Mind by Al Ries and Jack Trout—An all-time classic. For those new to the concept of branding, this book is a must read.

Ogilvy On Advertising by David Ogilvy—Also an advertising classic, the advertising concepts in this book have stood the test of time.

Write Great Ads by Erica Levy Klein—Even if you don't consider yourself a writer, Erica Levy Klein will have you writing effective marketing copy in no time.

Guerilla Publicity by Jay Conrad Levinson, Rick Frishman, Jill Lublin—Public relations has become an increasingly important part of marketing. This book will show you what you can do to gain valuable publicity for your business.

Building A Web Site For Dummies by David Crowder—An excellent book for a small business owner looking to establish an online presence.

Pay-Per-Click Search Engine Marketing Handbook by Boris Mordkovich, Eugene Mordovich—If you want to dip your toes into the world of pay-per-click advertising, this is a good place to start.

Other Books Of Note

The Brand Called You by Peter Montoya

The 22 Immutable Laws of Marketing by Al Ries and Laura Ries

The Copywriter's Handbook by Robert W. Bly

978-0-595-45098-5
0-595-45098-9